City Sounds

CRAIG BROWN

Greenwillow Books, New York

Pastels and pen-and-ink were used for the full-color art.
The text type is ITC Zapf International Medium.

Printed in Singapore by Tien Wah Press
First Edition
1 2 3 4 5 6 7 8 9 10

Library of Congress Cataloging-in-Publication Data

Brown, Craig McFarland.
City sounds/by Craig Brown.
p. cm.
Summary: Enumerates the many different sounds
a visitor might hear in the city, including the
honking of trucks, the sound of a jackhammer,
and the bonging of a big clock.
ISBN 0-688-10028-7 (trade)
ISBN 0-688-10029-5 (lib.).
1. City sounds—Juvenile literature.
2. City and town life—Juvenile literature.
[1. City sounds. 2. Sound.
3. City and town life.] I. Title.
HT 151.B76 1992
307.76—dc20
90-25632 CIP AC

For Susan

Farmer Brown came to the city.
He heard...

BBOOOOOOOOHHHHMMMMMM BOOOOOMMMM
the sound a tugboat makes.

HOOOOOOONNNN HHOONNNNNNN
the sound a train whistle makes.

Clickity clack clickity clack clickity clack
the sound the wheels make on the railroad track.

HOOOONNNNK HOOONNNNNK HOONK
the sound a truck makes.

Tweeeeeeeet tweeeeeeet tweeeeeet
the sound a whistle makes.

ERRRRRRRr ERRRRRRRRR ERRRRRRRRR
the sound a fire engine makes.

the sound a jackhammer makes.

rrRRr rrRRr rrRRr
the sound a police siren makes.

HHRRRUMMMMMM HRUMMMMM
the sound an excavator makes.

Trinnnngggh trilgggh tring
the sound a bicycle bell makes.

BOONNGG BOONNGG BOONNGG BOONNGG BOONNGG
the sound a clock makes.

Farmer Brown left the city
and drove home.